BACK TO BASICS

*Revisiting
Catholic Social Teaching*

CIIR

First published 1994

Catholic Institute for International Relations (CIIR)
Unit 3, Canonbury Yard, 190a New North Road, London N1 7BJ

© CIIR 1994

ISBN 1 85287 123 7

Printed in England by the Russell Press Ltd
Radford Mill, Norton Street, Nottingham NG7 3HN

Contents

Introduction	1
An organic tradition	2
Change of emphasis	6
Local Church: international voice	9
The political kingdom	12
The option for the poor	14
Workers and solidarity	15
Consultation or imposition?	18
Empowerment, confrontation or consensus?	19
Conclusion	21
Notes	24
Chronology	25

Back to Basics: Revisiting Catholic Social Teaching[1]

'According to me, at the root of many of the serious social and human problems besetting Europe and the world today are the distorted manifestations of capitalism. Of course, the capitalism of today is no longer the capitalism of Leo XIII's times. It has changed, and in good measure due to the influence of socialism.' Not the words of a young socialist but of an ageing Pope, John Paul II, speaking to a journalist in October 1993. Why do such remarks come as a suprise to many? How did the Catholic Church come by such views? Does the Church have any creative ideas that might contribute to solving the urgent problems facing society today?

The recognition of major political, socio-economic and ecological problems within capitalism, thrown sharply into focus by the collapse of communism in 1989, has put a premium on creative social thinking. So, while few today in the secular Northern industrialised world acknowledge the authority of the Church, many may wonder, sometimes in desperation, if it has new perspectives and solutions to offer. In the South such questions can be a matter of life and death. What follows seeks an answer to these questions and attempts to evaluate the significance of Catholic social teaching for the 1990s.

Introduction

The Church does indeed have something to say on social matters. Not exactly new ideas but some old ones that are still true and relevant. Yet there is a big gap between the Church's social teaching or doctrine, what it has said, and the lived reality of Church life, what it has done. This does not make the Church unique as an institution. But over the years, significant numbers of Church leaders seem not only to have ignored social teaching as expressed in official texts, but sometimes acted against their implementation.

Social doctrine and practice are the product of a developing vision of the Church's mission and how it should operate in the world. But this vision remains contested today within the Church, and christians appear on opposing sides in social and political conflicts. The periodic meetings of the bishops of Latin America witness these conflicts being fought out in debates about pastoral work and theology, or under the headings of 'human development' and 'culture'. Simplistic accounts of 'the Church's role in society' are thus invariably false. The Church is not a monolith.

Though a central part of the Church's moral guidance to christians and all people of good will, and in sharp contrast with its teaching on individual, sexual morality, Catholic social teaching receives little attention in the mass media and, with the exception of the *New Catechism*, in most programmes of catechetical instruction. Many christians talk as if sex alone is a legitimate object of moral concern, matters of social justice being relegated to an amoral realm of 'politics'. Often dubbed for this reason 'the Church's best kept secret', its social doctrine remains a closed book for many. This review aims to open the book not only for Catholics but for all those concerned with the contemporary social predicament.

An organic tradition

Catholic social teaching is often taken to mean the body of doctrine that began with Pope Leo XIII in the 1890s, texts emanating from Rome, or the sum total of authoritative pronouncements on social topics from bishops around the world. But such an approach begs many questions: how and whether such texts are 'received' by the christian community and acted upon, what historical context and political factors influenced their emphases and timing, and what conflicts they sought to resolve, or paper over? It inevitably neglects the more fundamental question: what in practice is the role of the Church in society and what is its social and political impact?

The thinking of the Church has been informed, of course, by far more than writings beginning in the last century. Indeed, these are best understood as an expression of the Church's corporate memory, of what it believed and believes. The early Church Fathers of the first christian centuries spoke passionately of *ta koina*, the common goods of the earth, and how they belonged to all, of the injustice of private ownership that neglects this principle. These are recurrent themes in religious life throughout the ages. 'Are you not a robber, you who make your own the things which you have received to distribute?' St Basil the Great wrote in the fourth century . . . 'That bread which you keep belongs to the hungry.' The same theme is reflected in a letter from the Pope John Paul II in the 1980s, *Dives in Misericordia*.

The wealth of the biblical tradition, only weakly expressed in the letters from Rome, awaited the 1960s, the second Vatican Council, and developments within the Latin American Church to be incorporated more fully into the mainstream of the Church's social thinking. When it did reappear, it was accompanied by the rich common experience of christians fighting against injustice, men and women who had begun reading the scriptures in the context of poverty and oppression. It put the central biblical theme of justice at the heart of christian life.

Whatever else the Church has stood for over the ages, it has set its face against individualism and chosen to speak of persons living in community.

The first fragments of a Catholic communitarian ethic in papal writings may be glimpsed in the 18th century. But this social emphasis was often associated with an authoritarian rejection of individual conscience that distinguished catholicism from most protestant ethics. The idea that 'error' had no rights lingered on and, up until the time of the UN Universal Declaration of Human Rights, Rome viewed the freedom to change religion, or reject religion, more as a concession than an inalienable right.

Catholic social teaching as a self-consciously evolving body of ideas began in 1891 with the publication of *Rerum Novarum* by Pope Leo XIII. Unlike Islam, in whose Shari'a Law most aspects of social life are regulated, this teaching has never sought to be — except arguably in the 1930s — a comprehensive blueprint for society. Rather it sets out principles, denounces aberrations and seeks to define human values that should be enshrined in social structures, in relations between nations, in war and peace, and in the conduct of individual states.

So it is that from 1891 until the early 1960s, a period during which the Church defined itself and lived with remarkable consistency as a closed hierarchical, sacramental institution, Catholic social teaching developed as an organic tradition. It was the doctrine of an institution that still saw itself as God's 'perfect society'[2] set against a sinful world. And it was some measure of this institution's self-absorption that it took decades after the industrial revolution swept across Europe, carrying with it Marx's analysis of political economy, before the Church saw fit to speak out. In some ways its two principal themes were reactions to industrialisation and the modern state: the protection of the poor and powerless in society with, as a corollary, a denunciation of political systems that denied them this protection. The defence of particular rights of the family, especially to own private property and — for the breadwinner — to a just wage and trade union protection, was championed against unregulated capitalism and communist collectivism.

To some extent the principal rights demanded of the state reflected the Church's special interests: freedom for it to administer the sacraments, the right of the Church to educate youth and inform public opinion about morality, and the need for citizens to obey lawful authority. These were the means that the Church required to fulfill its work of salvation in the world. It saw their defence not so much as a struggle to retain its institutional power — though it was that — than as legitimate demands stemming from the Church's very nature. It found particular difficulties with totalitarian states because, by definition, they also attempted to be 'perfect societies' in the technical sense, in competition with the Church, and in so doing set out to deprive the Church of the means that it required to achieve its goals.

Since the Church saw its roots as being in the family, the basic unit of society, it was acutely sensitive to social, economic and political forces that disrupted family life. The rights of workers to form trade unions, receive a decent family wage and resist oppressive conditions within the law were all proclaimed. Mothers had an obligation to care for their children at home. Governments, in turn, had the duty to seek the 'common good' and help the weak and poor. In Britain Cardinal Manning was a powerful advocate of these principles, speaking out on the rights of the poor and the failures of capitalism, and arbitrating in the 1889 dock strike to the consternation of the Catholic establishment.

After the Russian revolution, the Church's teaching remained reactive, with a vision of society based on interlocking sets of duties and rights. It reflected two opposing fears: the disintegration of society as a result of class conflict, and the growth of overpowerful states, more especially on the totalitarian model of Stalinism. The concept of subsidiarity, that no higher social formation should arrogate to itself functions that can be performed efficiently by a lower one, grew out of this fear of totalitarianism. And the family was seen as the most fundamental of the 'subsidiary' units in society.

These fears were justified. Mussolini took control of education in Italy and destroyed the movements of Catholic university students and scouts as well as the *Partido Popolare*. Pope Pius XI responded with *Divini Illius Magistri* asserting the primacy of the family and the primacy of the Church in education, the former by natural right, the latter by divine ordinance. Soviet communism aimed no less to root itself in the family through the education of youth. But repression was more brutal. The influence of the Church was effectively eliminated from society by the coercive atheism of the state and confiscation of Church property. The little Catholic Church in Moscow, even in the late 1980s, was a remarkable symbol of the past, cowering between the vast blocks of the Lubianka with KGB cameras trained on the Church porch.

The Spanish Civil War and the 'Catholic' rebellion in Mexico[3] further provoked the Church into forging a tradition in opposition to the left. But this was associated in *Quadragesimo Anno* with strong reservations about liberal capitalism and leanings towards a corporatist vision of society. Pope Pius XI sought a model of society based on professional and vocational groups that cut across class lines, a 'Third Way', in some respects a return to the organic society of the Middle Ages. As a footnote to these events, in Britain the Sword of the Spirit, the precursor of CIIR, was started in 1940 as an antidote to the flirtation of some English Catholic intellectuals with the idea of a fascist international order. Other priests in Rome, quite literally shoved off the pavement by Mussolini's thugs, drew different conclusions about fascism. One of them, Bishop Donal Lamont, applied it in his opposition to the Smith regime in Rhodesia 30 years later. It was the subsequent horrors, and then defeat, of Nazi Germany that caused Catholic intellectual and clerical protagonists of fascism to back away.

But in Spain and Portugal, including its colonies and, of course, in parts of Latin America, the Church retained a working alliance with fascist governments until their defeat in the 1980s.

To some extent, then, the 1930s proved a transitional period in the Church's social teaching. The possibility of a 'Third Way', between unrestrained capitalism and the arch-enemy communism, reached its nadir in the ruins of Nazi Germany. It rose again later, only constrained and 'semi-detached', in the form of christian democracy. Meanwhile, in the vigour of its corporatist vision, first seen in *Rerum Novarum*, the Church had gone back to the Middle Ages in more ways than one; it once again conceded the right of rebellion against tyrannical government that had been lost sight of in the fearful aftermath of the French and Russian revolutions.

Though Catholics and communists fought alongside each other and sometimes against each other — in the war against nazism, Church organisations operating in civil society were still officially blessed as much for being organised opponents of communist and socialist counterparts, as protagonists for a specific Catholic social agenda. Christian democracy was supported either openly or quietly as a proper political manifestation of Catholicism. In Australia participation in the Labour Party divided the Church. In Netherlands, Belgium, France, Switzerland, Italy, Austria and Quebec, Catholic trade union groups grew up and were encouraged while, around the world, Catholics were officially discouraged from participating in national democratic movements with strong socialist or communist influence. The right of workers to form a trade union often had become narrowed in practice to the right to set up rival christian trade unions, and thereby often to split the worker movement.

On the other hand, those reared in the 'see-judge act' method[1] of the Belgian Canon Joseph Cardijn, in movements such as Young Christian Students and Young Christian Workers, explored a class analysis of society and often took up radical positions on matters of social and economic justice. The movements had begun as associations of christian workers in Brussels in 1926 but rapidly spread to Paris and, by 1930, included youth in a number of different sectors, workers, students, sailors, farmers, as well as middle class groups. These movements were later to play a catalytic role in the Church in many Third World countries, and to influence post-war European politics.

The surge of socialist expectation aroused during the Second World War found little echo amongst the Church leadership in Britain. The principles of Catholic social teaching could encompass the idea of state pensions and state-run primary education, pressed for family allowances, but baulked at other aspects of the welfare state like a free health service, and at any state monopoly of secondary education.

Back to Basics

Almost by default, Pope Pius XII accepted liberal capitalism, which was going into a sustained period of growth towards the end of his pontificate. From his perspective in Europe, it seemed to offer the only option to combat poverty and safeguard freedom. The right to private property had become almost an absolute right, untempered by the ancient concept of the 'common good'. He moved swiftly to crush the worker-priest movement in France, which had taken priests into industrial chaplaincy as workers. Several had assumed roles as shop stewards and become militant, politically conscious champions of workers' rights. As far as colonialism was concerned, the Church followed events more opportunistically than prophetically, relatively silent in the early stages of anti-colonial nationalism, speaking out by 1957 in *Fidei Donum* on the right of colonised people to their independence. Younger mission clergy increasingly identified with more radical nationalist elements in their aspirations, as the first generation of indigenous clergy began to react against racist and paternalist authority in colonial state and Church respectively. In Latin America, the Brazilian bishops led by Dom Helder Câmara held their first small national conference in 1952, and in 1955 the bishops of the continent began meeting for the first time to consider the state of Church and society, beginning a process that was to have dramatic consequences a decade later. In Africa local clergy were rapidly being made bishops. In China the process of indigenisation was well underway.[5] The Church's leadership was becoming more internationalist.

Change of emphasis

An international, ecumenical Church in the pluralist world of the 1960s could only be described with some difficulty as a 'perfect society'. Pope John XXIII, by calling a second Vatican Council, brought about a redefinition of the Church that was to have profound consequences in the realm of Catholic social thought and action. Instead of a 'perfect society', primarily turned in on its sacramental life, centralised and defensive, the Council put forward a vision of the Church as an international community open to the world, seeking the spirit of God in it, sharing the optimism, and the sufferings, of the age. This vision was reflected in Pope John's two major social encyclicals, *Mater et Magistra* and *Pacem in Terris*.

As a Vatican diplomat, Pope John XXIII may have glimpsed how the wealthy and powerful had manipulated Catholic social teaching, turning it into an ideology in its own right in the combat with communism. In *Mater et Magistra* and *Pacem in Terris*, he dissociated himself from this process in a change of emphasis that was to be continued by later popes. Henceforth the right to private property was more clearly balanced by the demands of the 'common good', and references to the equitable distribution of the world's resources, 'the universal destiny' of material goods and wealth, became more insistent and frequent a theme.

He likewise seemed able to rise above a blind fear of communism — perhaps because Nikita Khrushchev had distanced himself from Stalinism and held out hope of change. He went so far as to distinguish between 'false philosophical theories' and the 'historical movements' that drew their inspiration from them. Moreover, while retaining the principle of subsidiarity, he was willing to accept much greater levels of state intervention, compatible with the welfare state and forms of social democracy. It might not have been politically an 'opening to the left' but it was certainly a distancing from the right.

Despite the mythology that came to surround him, Pope John XXIII was not a radical thinker. He was a gradualist in matters of social change, and he retained an understandable but incorrect belief that capitalism could bring Western levels of wealth to the Third World. In a remarkable way he demonstrated the continuities in Catholic social thought while having the vision that pointed the Church on a new compass bearing.

As the Council opened in October 1962, in the midst of the Cuban missile crisis, the assembled bishops in their message to the world spoke of two urgent topics, peace and social justice. Henceforth the Church was to link the two repeatedly, seeing justice as the necessary condition for a stable peace within and between nations. In the preface to *Gaudium et Spes*, produced three years later[6] and addressed to this dangerous new world, they signalled the new vision: 'The joys and the hopes, the griefs and the anxieties of the people of this age, especially those who are poor or in any way afflicted, these are the joys and the hopes, the griefs and the anxieties of the followers of Christ.' Together with calls for more equitable terms of global trade, for aid and investment in underdeveloped countries, and respect for their cultures, this showed that relations between the North and South of the world were now a pressing issue for the Church.

This North-South theme marked a significant shift away from the narrow focus on Europe of the past, and it was followed up by perhaps the most innovative of all the papal documents produced in the 1960s, *Populorum Progressio* (the Progress of Peoples), from Pope Paul VI. It is here that the concept of 'integral development' is fleshed out: the realisation of the fullness of human potential, respectful of culture, which rejects the reduction of development to mere economic growth.

This definition of what it means to be human, in which development is seen as a process of becoming 'more human', implicitly refutes any distinction between 'missionary work' and 'development work'. The two fundamental goals of the Church's mission are summed up by the word 'evangelisation'. So literacy and basic education are seen as important, both because they enable people, specifically, to read the Bible, and

7

because, generally, they enable people to develop their full human potential. These themes are elaborated more fully in *Evangelii Nuntiandi*.

Equally important, the encyclical sets out the idea of structural change as a necessary condition for global social justice. Pope Paul VI speaks of 'bold transformations' being required in economic systems and points out that free trade, 'taken by itself is no longer able to govern international relations'. A brief and cautious critique of neo-colonialism is accompanied by a denunciation of privileged national elites who hold a monopoly of power. His insight that economic domination is a significant cause of the problems of the Third World leads him to advocate some form of regulatory world body. In this internationalist vision, Pope Paul VI was remarkably in tune with the progressive thought of his times, his ideas reflected in the South's later demands for a new international economic order.

These insights are developed more radically by the world's bishops in 1971 — when they began meeting regularly in the form of a synod under papal direction — with an explicit rejection of 'trickle-down' development. They speak of 'the hope . . . that it would be possible to feed the hungry at least from the crumbs falling from the table, but this has proved a vain hope in underdeveloped areas and in pockets of poverty in wealthy areas', a point made by Cardinal Manning about the British poor almost a century before. In addition they point to the disastrous ecological consequences if the Western model of development is taken up by the rest of the world.

The 1960s were a significant period of transition in the Church's social teaching as they were in many aspects of social life around the world. In the 19th century thinking of Pope Leo XIII, social doctrine was largely deduced from the first principles of Greek and Roman stoic 'natural law' philosophy, and derived from the thought of the 13th century Dominican theologian, Thomas Aquinas,[7] widely taught in Catholic seminaries. In 1963, in *Pacem in Terris*, this philosophy is used to great effect as a basis for an extended discussion of human rights — for the first time in Church teaching. Human rights were 'read off' what it meant to be human; religious freedom stemmed, as an inalienable right, from the dignity of the human person. The same human rights theme is taken up again by Pope John Paul II in *Redemptor Hominis*.

But after the Vatican Council social teaching begins to move out of a natural law framework. It is increasingly derived from the Church's vision of evangelisation, described by the world's bishops in their 1971 synod as having action on behalf of social justice and transformation of the world as a constitutive dimension. In other words, for the Church to do its job properly it must be in the midst of the human struggle for justice and development. For example, in *Evangelii Nuntiandi* Pope Paul VI says in 1975: 'One cannot dissociate the plan of creation from the plan of redemption. The latter plan touches the very concrete situations of injustice to be combated and of justice to be restored.' For creation, read 'the way things are made' or, in traditional Catholic terms, 'the order of nature', and for redemption read 'the way God wants them to be' or 'the order of grace'.

In short, the Church no longer presented social teaching mainly as the product of a philosophy that might be challenged like any other human construct. Now it appears in a more integral way as part of the gospel message, the Good News it was divinely mandated to teach. It was basic to the Church's mission. It lay at the heart of its pastoral ministry, so the idea that there was another 'spiritual' task unconnected to it, which might be posited against it, was not the mind of the Church. To make this teaching more authentic the Church openly spoke in *Gaudium et Spes* of giving up its own privileges afforded by the state and, at the 1971 Synod of Bishops, of the need for justice in the Church. The former led in turn to the formation of the Pontifical Commission for Justice and Peace, and SODEPAX, a short-lived ecumenical endeavour with the World Council of Churches focused on justice and development.

So the Church, by moving away from abstract thinking about the nature of humanity, was led into focusing on 'concrete situations' in social analysis, and reflecting on them theologically in its social teaching. Concrete situations were, of course, the particular local and national contexts for the Church's work, and these, in turn, were influenced by wider economic forces. This was particularly stressed in the encyclical *Octogesima Adveniens*. As a result, local Churches and bishops' conferences in different countries were able to make their own unique contribution to the universal Church by analysis and reflection on their 'reality'.

These were potentially big steps, drawing the Church into local cultures and socio-economic contexts and into a new self-critical awareness. In the light of christian support for democratic struggles in society, it raised the question of democracy in the Church. Church and state met less as two negotiating 'powers' in a formal *Concordat*, and more in a dialogue between two different moral cultures. In its task of social transformation and work for justice, the Church was not self-sufficient; it needed all the help it could get.

Local Church: International voice

A dominant theme at the second Vatican Council had been the tempering of the hierarchical, centralised nature of the Catholic Church with more 'horizontal' emphases, 'collegiality' referring to the relationship between bishops and pope, and 'the people of God' referring to the Church as a whole, particularly the 'laity'. Both suggested what might be described as a devolution of authority and corresponded to the essentially liberal ecclesiastical agenda of the Churches in the industrialised North, with their rich dioceses and articulate middle class Catholics.[8] Coupled with the vision contained in *Gaudium et Spes* and *Populorum Progressio*, this created the necessary conditions for, and released, an unparalleled creative upsurge in the life of the Church. In the North, Catholic development agencies started up; in the South, christians, often reared in the Cardijn see-judge-act method, moved with a new confidence into urban and peasant community organisations, development projects and popular movements. By the early 1970s justice and peace groups were starting up around the world, often in the teeth of opposition from conservative bishops and clergy, despite Pope Paul VI's clear call for their formation.

This upsurge reached a 'critical mass' in Latin America. Widespread poverty, the thinking of the Brazilian popular educator, Paulo Freire, the work of a few liberation theologians like the Peruvian, Gustavo Gutiérrez, the reaction to oppression by oligarchies and their military backers, and the strong underpinning of a popular Catholic culture relatively uncontested by other religious forces combined to produce in 1968 the remarkable event of the Medellín conference. At this meeting of the bishops of Latin America, attended by Pope Paul VI, things were said and documents produced that were to have a lasting impact not only on the region but on the universal Church.

Previous papal documents had been characterised by a Euro-centric approach, a caution in criticism of unregulated capitalism and a top-down vision of how social change came about. At best a tentative suggestion was made that structural change had to be added to personal 'change of heart' if things were to alter. But at Medellín the bishops forged a tradition in Latin America that was altogether more radical and forthright. Most notably Medellín brought into the Church's discourse on society resonant words from the life of those working with and amongst the poor of the continent. 'Liberation' rather than 'development' became the catchword. Development was a word sullied by the experience of President Kennedy's Alliance for Progress programme that resulted in the distribution of wealth in Latin American society becoming even more skewed. 'Conscientisation', with its political overtones, superseded 'education for economic progress'. There was also a passing reference to 'institutional violence' in the context of the injustice inherent in certain political and economic structures. This threw back the idea that the source of violence was amongst the poor.

The bishops also in effect gave explicit permission for the continued growth of a 'poor Church' that adopted poverty as 'the condition of the needy of the world in order to bear witness to the evil which it represents'. This Church would be able to denounce and analyse poverty and injustice from within, because it would not be blinded by the ideology of the rich and their dominant culture.

In the decade after Medellín, however, the 'poor Church' about which they spoke might equally well have been described as a 'Church of the Poor', with its structures of basic christian communities, its methodology of reflection on the Bible in the light of the experience of poverty, and its intellectuals and liberation theology. With the exception of Brazil, only a small minority of Church leaders and educators in practice supported this way of 'being Church'. It was, and remained, tolerated rather than supported, more often kept at a distance and opposed by the rich. It became the 'Church of the Poor' not because it was divisive and wanted to separate from bishops and the rich, but because many of the latter had refused to become a 'poor Church' as Medellín had advocated.

The Medellín conference took place as liberation movements around the world were taking up armed struggle against injustice and what they labelled 'US imperialism'. The bishops believed that the costs of armed struggle against the Latin American dictatorships would be unacceptably high, with no guarantee of success. But they did not declare themselves opposed to violence on principle. Nor were they willing to declare openly that violent confrontation with the rich, powerful, landowners and military *would* be necessary, however much they were explicit that advocacy of 'conscientisation' necessarily entailed some confrontation short of armed struggle. They even disarmingly suggested that public officials needed the organisation of popular movements in order to implement social projects. The Latin American Church remained far from unified in its social thinking, so Medellín was unable to forge a unified social policy.

Many of the bishops were most comfortable with the politics of multi-class alliances and thus favoured christian democracy as the 'correct' politics for Catholics. The bishops' dilemmas reflected those of christian democracy — with its need for middle class support and ambiguous relationship with the poor in Latin America. Their continuing stress on non-confrontational ways forward was, in part, tactical but it did not amount to a realistic programme of action. In parliamentary democracies, and with respect for civil society and human rights, consensus strategies might have offered a way forward. In Latin America in the 1970s they did not.

In reality, attempts at managing social change by retaining a consensus model while supporting popular movements, which were bound to confront power in one way or another, amounted to two incompatible policies. Such divergent tactics bedevilled a coherent strategy of social change. At times they resulted in a stop-go approach to social action by the Catholic community. In Chile the price of incoherence was very high: only a minority of the Church supported Salvador Allende's Popular Unity government and some bishops went along with Pinochet's 1973 coup. It was to run into the buffers in Nicaragua, South Africa and El Salvador, and was briefly replaced. But in most places around the world the consensus model was retained, causing frustration, misunderstanding and haemorrhaging of politically active christians from Church life into secular community or national politics.

The political kingdom

The Medellín conference, and the preference for the poor expressed at it, rang bells throughout the Third World when liberation theologians, and religious orders, began to disseminate its conclusions in the course of the 1970s. It offered a different vision of the Church, alongside and accompanying the poor who were, in faith, the 'new subjects of history'. The 'Church of the Poor' flowered in these years. But in the eyes of its detractors, and necessarily its defenders, it opened up the vexed question of the Church's relationship to politics.

In *Octogesima Adveniens* Pope Paul VI confronts this issue and acknowledges openly that the Church's social teaching, if it is to enter the realm of solutions rather than rhetoric, must enter the political domain. He recognises that economic and social questions are 'felt to be' — the caution of an old and tired man — ultimately questions of political power, and he is clear that passing to the political dimension 'also expresses a demand made by people today for a greater share in the exercice of authority and in consultation for decision-making'.

The 1971 synod of bishops, in the same year, emphasises that the core of the problem of injustice is the marginalisation of people, the concentration of power and the failure to ensure popular participation in decision-making. But there was no move made by Church leadership to engage constructively with the Marxist tradition. Pope Paul VI, ironically in the light of his successor's later support for Solidarnosc in Poland, explicitly warns against the politicisation of trade unions, such is his concern to avoid implicating the Church in divisive social strategies based on class conflict.[9]

The rise of movements like 'Christians for Socialism' in Latin America that moved far to the left of conventional christian democracy, the participation of christians in Latin American liberation movements and the success of Marxist-inspired nationalist forces in Cuba, Vietnam, Angola and Mozambique, with the subsequent exodus of Church personnel who had opposed the insurgents, increased the level of anxiety among the Church leadership during the 1970s. Many feared that the trajectory of Medellín would carry the Church into realms where contamination with the virus of Marxist ideology was inevitable.

The safe shell of christian democracy virtually imploded in Latin America during the 1970s. Allende's electoral victory in 1970 and the subsequent Pinochet coup in Chile was one measure of this failure. The

Revisiting Catholic Social Teaching

victory of the Sandinista revolution in Nicaragua at the end of the decade, with many pious Catholics in the guerrilla army, seemed to focus anxiety, as it did the obsessive, violent opposition of the United States. By bringing radical priests into government, it brought the problem home to conservatives in the Latin American hierarchy, already worried by the proliferation of basic christian communities. The level of tension in the Church ratcheted up.

This was the context in which preparations for the follow-up conference to Medellín, held in Mexico at Puebla, took place. Pope Paul VI was dead and a Polish Pope, three months after his election — unexpectedly brought on by the tragic death of Pope John Paul I — found himself in January 1979 thrown into the ferment of the Latin American Church. At stake were two visions of the Church, one growing out of the new directions of the second Vatican Council, open to the world, committed to a pastoral preference for the poor, the other seeking a 'purification' of the Church that would return it to the narrowly spiritual, fearful that the Church of the Poor and its theology had become an instrument in alien political projects for society.

To some extent a few liberation theologians had played into the hands of those seeking to clothe their comfortable co-existence with oppressive oligarchies and the military with theological respectability. They had too eagerly adopted the slogan of Ghana's Marxist president, Kwame Nkrumah, 'seek first the political kingdom', to the point of instrumentalising the gospel message. The imperatives of the political struggle for justice had led to a neglect of the spirituality of justice that flowered around the world in the 1980s. But the many were tarred with the omissions of the few, both in the lists of names targeted by the intelligence services of the Latin American armies, that failed to discriminate between the wide variety of 'liberation theologians', and in the propaganda success of the conservatives in falsely equating the theology and practice of the Church of the Poor with Marxism. The vast majority were simply applying the gospel to their times and context.

The new Pope was a trained moral philosopher. His political experience had been of resistance to nazism and to years of bureaucratic communism in Poland. At Puebla he reaffirmed that action for justice was an essential part of evangelistion, while warning against Christ being reduced to a 'political' figure. But he could do little more than hold the ring in a polarised Church. He seemed uncertain what direction to take. Only in the mid-1980s did he begin charting a more determined course.

The Puebla conference began a process that was to be repeated at the next Latin American bishops' meeting in Santo Domingo in October 1992. Because of the opposition of the conservatives, it was not possible to elaborate the new vision of the Church as far as it concerned change in internal Church life and organisation. Even superficial change in the structures of the Church meant an assault on the Holy of Holies. Change

13

in how the Church interacted with the world was a terrain which was less heavily defended by conservative bishops. So things were tactically fought out, as if they were once removed, in the realm of 'pastoral practice' or in what has been called 'christian anthropology' and 'human development', in other words, how the Church does its job in the world and what it believes being human means.

In the pontificate of John Paul II the latter was developed and elaborated as a form of 'integral humanism' which saw the spiritual as the deepest dimension of human 'material' being. But he proved to be, and remains, adamantly opposed to any change in the internal ordering of the Church. What the Church did, its goals, had in significant ways been redefined but the means of achieving these goals, Catholic education, training of clergy, the defined roles of religious, priests, bishops and the Roman Curia remained unchanged, jealously guarded. Thus, though Catholic action on behalf of justice developed and grew, bringing with it a renewed spirituality, the Church in its structures remained officially fixed in aspic.

The option for the poor

For this reason, the decade after Puebla saw two contradictory tendencies gather force. On the one hand, the Puebla conference ratified the vision of Medellín and made it explicit in a phrase that was to characterise a transformation of Church life and resonate around the world: 'the option for the poor'. The key sentence in the final document is: 'We affirm the need for conversion on the part of the whole Church to a preferential option for the poor, an option aimed at their integral liberation.' It spoke of the scandalous reality of 'economic imbalances' and called for the construction of a 'just and free society'. Far from abandoning the rich, though: 'the witness of a poor Church can evangelise the rich whose hearts are attached to wealth, thus converting and freeing them from this bondage and their own egotism'. The poor had become evangelisers in official thinking.

Nothing could be clearer than that. But while this was being worked out in practice, as religious orders and christians adopted 'the option for the poor', in shantytowns and refugee camps, among people living with Aids, with street children, in the struggle against apartheid, with oppressed indigenous peoples, in the decayed inner cities of the industrialised North, Rome was appointing bishops to vacant dioceses who, on the whole, seemed to be chosen for their capacity to hold the line on change in the Church. Often, but not always, such men were out of sympathy with the Church of the Poor, its theology and life; sometimes they seem to have been deliberately chosen to curtail its activities. In Brazil, the champions of this Church, the architects of pastoral plans to realise 'the preferential option', like Dom Helder Câmara or Cardinal Arns, seemed targeted by the Vatican for special attention designed to limit and block their work.

Not suprisingly, the contradictions became focused on liberation theology and its proponents. Liberation theologians were harassed by the Vatican, their writings scrutinised with almost the rigour of a state censor, and one or two who were disinclined to bend before the hot winds coming from Rome forced to renounce their priesthood. The conflict found its historic symbol in 1983 as an angry Pope admonished a Sandinista priest on the tarmac of Managua airport, and shouted 'silence' at a papal mass to a Nicaraguan congregation. They had been calling for him to acknowledge the presence of mothers of soldiers killed in the US-promoted Contra war against Nicaragua.

The hierarchy of the Brazilian Church bore much of the force of this assault but skillfully defused it. In 1984 the Vatican issued an *Instruction on Certain Aspects of 'Liberation Theology'* that showed no sympathy or even close acquaintance with the reality of the Church of the Poor and its theology, and seemed to view it as an abstract doctrine replete with errors. Widely believed to be the work of Cardinal Ratzinger, a liberal turned conservative, it was followed two years later with an *Instruction on Christian Freedom and Liberation*, which bore the marks of the pope's closer involvement. In the interim the Brazilian bishops and others had been clarifying matters.

The second document, while not a resounding endorsement, made it clear that liberation theology was thoroughly within the mainstream of Christian thought and reiterated many of its themes. There followed what amounted to a stand-off. Henceforth the debate left the highly visible arena of written instructions and returned to a low intensity war of attrition fought out in seminaries, episcopal appointments, and allocation of funds and personnel. Any idea that some kind of truce had been achieved was finally dispelled when the bishops of Latin America and the Caribbean began preparations for their next meeting in Santo Domingo ten years later.

Workers and solidarity

It is against this background that the extraordinarily prolific and, at times, innovative, contribution of Pope John Paul II to social teaching needs to be considered. He set out to solve a number of problems which he saw arising from the Church's organic tradition: firstly how to cope using a personalist philosophy[10] with the impersonal nature of 'structural injustice', how to deal with the conflict between christians who sought consensus and those who saw conflict as the only way forward in the quest for justice, or put more in terms of his local experience, what to substitute for class conflict at the heart of Catholic social thought, and how to integrate theology and social doctrine.

In *Sollicitudo Rei Socialis*, published in early 1988, 'structures of injustice', the term used in Catholic social analysis, becomes 'structures of sin', making economic and political conduct fall irrevocably into the deeper dimension and category of morality and theology. He spells it out: 'Hidden behind certain decisions, apparently only inspired by economics and politics, are real forms of idolatry: of money, ideology, class, technology.' This biblical reference to idolatry is the gravest possible charge as it means worship of false gods; the pope describes these gods as a thirst for power and desire for profit totally lacking in moral constraint.

John Paul II, fearful of Marxist forms of structural analysis, emphasises that it is through 'concrete acts' rooted in 'personal sin' that structures of sin come into being, and are reproduced in subsequent generations. Structures for the pope are determined by persons, never the other — Marxist — way round. Liberation theologians like Gustavo Gutiérrez see 'integral liberation' as a many-sided process involving the personal and the structural in a complex interaction. But it seems to be a one-way street for Pope John Paul II. Nothing must dilute individual responsibility.

This gives him a theoretical headache in a number of his writings. In his earlier 1981 encyclical on work, *Laborem Exercens*, he uses the idea of the 'indirect employer' as a heuristic device to explain how it can be that economic structures force 'direct' employers of labour to pay inhuman wages in the Third World. Thus terms of trade between North and South, Third World debt, European Community agricultural policy, can all indirectly determine that a worker is not given a living wage, or, as the pope puts it, become 'an occasion for various forms of exploitation or injustice and as a result influence the labour policy of individual states'. The point that he clearly wishes to underline is that christians, through global economic structures and international relations, are implicated in, and are even complicit in, injustices that at first sight appear not to be their personal moral responsibility. But the point is that they participate as 'indirect employers' no less culpably at times than the direct employer of sweated labour in the Third World. If this seems a tortuous explanation it is because the pope needs an 'indirect person' as a cause for structural sin.

As Archbishop of Cracow, Pope John Paul II had produced a work of personalist philosophy in 1969 in which he elaborated a concept of solidarity. In it he sees solidarity as an attitude to other people that refuses to instrumentalise 'the other' and is open to self-sacrifice on behalf of the neighbour. Obviously influenced by the context of Catholic resistance to Polish state communism, it saw solidarity as the necessary moral condition for building community, and, not suprisingly, includes in the concept the possibility of opposition and dissent. He was later to find the expression of such dissent on moral issues within the Church both burdensome and

Revisiting Catholic Social Teaching

reprehensible. But his personalism provided a basis for evaluating political systems. It contained radical elements and shared, in places, the insights of Marx.

The solidarity theme emerges strongly in *Laborem Exercens* where he speaks of the need for 'new movements of solidarity of workers' and of the struggle for justice by workers in trade unions. In *Sollicitudo* he more extensively carries the concept onto the plane of international relations and provides some pithy definitions of solidarity as a virtue: not a transient feeling but 'a firm and persevering determination to commit oneself to the common good', describing it as the moral response to the reality of global interdependence.

The basis of 'integral humanism' behind the Pope's thinking, that the human person was the measure of work, economic systems and politics, meant that his encyclicals tended to criticise communism and liberal capitalism even-handedly in the first decade of his pontificate. In *Sollicitudo* he contrasts the consumerism and waste of the industrialised North, which he calls 'superdevelopment', with the 'underdevelopment' of the South. He uses the term 'fourth world' to describe the poor of the capitalist North. He roundly places capital at the service of labour and not vice-versa. So much so that *Sollicitudo* was openly criticised by right-wing Catholics and in editorials of the right-wing press. But in *Centesimus Annus*, published in May 1991, a much more ambiguous tone is adopted. In what appears to be an attack on the welfare state, but may have merely been a call for more social participation in it to eliminate dependency, those on the right of politics were given potential ammunition.

But his writing by then had returned to the general prescriptions of the organic tradition; the market economy was the best of bad economic systems, it required a 'strong juridical framework which places it at the service of human freedom', and it had to be 'appropriately controlled by the forces of society and by the state so as to guarantee that the basic needs of the whole of society are satisfied'. Unadultered liberal capitalism, what he later calls 'savage' capitalism, was morally unacceptable without these minimum conditions being fulfilled. In the context of a shift to the right in European politics — though only in this context — such prescriptions could seem radical.

Unlike Pius XI, Pope John Paul was not in the business of offering alternative political models, which was just as well because at the time there did not appear to be any. Nor had he much time for Italian christian democracy, from whose corruption he had suffered, and which was on the point of disintegration as a political force. He described Third Way formulas in 1993 as 'utopian' and unrealisable.

Centesimus Annus, with its extended personal reflection on the events of 1989, highlighted how much Pope John Paul's global vision was rooted in his own experience of eastern Europe. The financial and human resources available to Solidarnosc through the Church and CIA contributed substantially to the vigour of Solidarnosc in the 1980s. And Solidarnosc undoubtedly played a catalytic role in the unravelling of Soviet hegemony in eastern Europe, and the linked disintegration of the Soviet Union. His understanding of the Church's role in this process, though, seems exaggerated but not to the point of triumphalism.

But for the Latin American bishops gathered in Santo Domingo in November 1992, the problem was not communism but the growing impoverishment of the vast majority of their people under the impact of neo-liberalism, the demands of indigenous peoples for their rights, and the struggle for land. For the African bishops preparing for their 1994 synod the problem was the destitution of their continent, the arms trade and the assault on their cultures. While most of the world's one billion Roman Catholics might have shared, at a notional level, the Pope's sense of the fall of communism as an epochal event, in their lives other matters assumed greater significance.

Consultation or imposition?

During the 1980s, the premise that democratically structured consultation was important to any 'integral humanism' seeped into Church life and influenced even the top-down practice of the local Church. The 1980 Pastoral Congress in Britain, despite the bishops' subsequent failure to take up its challenges seriously, was a tangible expression of the mood. In South Africa the non-racial democratic movement created an ethos in which the bishops' conference was more-or-less open to outsiders and inputs from socially committed lay activists. Radical theologians began to 'do theology with the people' in a way reminiscent of the Latin American basic christian communities, reflecting on their analysis of the crisis in apartheid, and creating a radical 'contextual theology'. In the United States the bishops engaged in extensive processes of structured consultation with a wide variety of relevant people and experts before producing in 1983 a letter on peace and disarmament and, in 1986, on economic justice. Although the influence of Rome has to be factored in to the results of these US consultations — the Vatican dissuaded the US bishops from rejecting nuclear deterrence out of hand — consultation undoubtedly accounted for the outstandingly pertinent reflections on key social issues that resulted.

More importantly, they began to result in the bishops, and indirectly Rome, being challenged on areas of concern, like the marginalisation of women and the environment which they had ideological reasons to avoid (the former for obvious reasons, the latter because the inherited 17th century distortions of the Judaeo-Christian tradition, and 'person-centred'

Revisiting Catholic Social Teaching

development, did not lend themselves easily to a discourse on ecology). A number of different bishops' conferences, most notably those of the Philippines and the European bishops in a joint statement with the Council of European (Protestant) Churches in Basle, have since made radical statements on ecology, calling in the latter case for a 'complete reversal of the concept of sustained economic growth'. The pope produced a document on the dignity and equality of women in 1988, and in his 1990 message on World Peace Day, developed the theme of 'the integrity of creation' to condemn the plundering of natural resources.

The meeting of the bishops of Latin America and the Caribbean in Santo Domingo in October 1992 was preceded by widespread consultation. The Vatican attempted to change the agenda and reject the Santo Domingo preparatory documents. Though many strong sections, calling for the Church to support the struggle for democracy and land rights, and making their own the thinking of indigenous people about the land and ecology, survived into the final document, others were lost or subtly changed, particularly those on women.

More importantly, the conduct of the Latin American conservatives and Vatican officials, who attempted to hijack the conference, provided a lesson in the authoritarianism and centralising mode of Church life envisioned by Rome. Even middle-of-the-road bishops could not see how such a vision, which smacked of the petty bureaucratic control of an old eastern bloc state, could be compatible with the values set out in the Church's social teaching. Such a top-down, centralised Church simply disqualified itself from the tasks set out in its texts on social justice. The means precluded the end.

Empowerment, confrontation or consensus?

The weakness of Catholic social teaching is, of course, that it ends where questions of methodology begin. This allows methods that cannot possibly achieve the stated or desired social end, or rectify the abuse condemned, to be advocated and justified from some a priori assumption about what is, or is not, a christian approach to social justice.

An avoidance of confrontation at all costs is not a christian principle, nor is consensus. The superficial unity of a divided Church is not to be equated with its 'oneness', nor is it a value that overrides the simple demands of justice; the martyrdom of Archbishop Oscar Romero of San Salvador is a profound example of this gospel truth. Such assumptions often ignore the life and practice of Jesus himself, or wilfully distort his sayings, taking them out of context, to justify actions taken on entirely different grounds. 'Render unto Caesar' is a canny response to a trick question, but Jesus' audience would have heard his reply as relativising the claims of the imperial 'state'. It is, of course, most frequently used in the opposite sense to bolster the claims of the state.

But, as fragments of papal speeches around the world indicate, the option for the poor necessarily and properly leads to the empowerment of the poor, so that the poor make their own option for liberation/salvation. This may threaten both state and institutional Church. Pope John Paul quite clearly recognised this in eastern Europe where it had apparently negligible consequences for internal Church structure and discipline, but has had difficulty in Latin America where the opposite appeared to be the case. And in such empowerment, confrontation often cannot be avoided. A country like Haiti, with a priest and liberation theologian as legal president, and confrontation between a majority and a tiny corrupt elite, thus emerges as a worst-case scenario as the Vatican and a majority of Haitian bishops show themselves willing to co-exist with a government of military thugs and work against a democratically elected president, Jean-Bertrand Aristide.

But in less extreme instances, Church leaders' vagueness about method — apart from a precise rejection of violence — has allowed ways to be found of co-existing comfortably with forms of fascism and forms of individualistic liberal capitalism with negligible resistance. Such an acceptance of collusive co-existence stems from a judgement that these political systems permit the Church to carry out its divinely appointed task, and to achieve enough of its proclaimed goals, for the relationship to be considered tolerable, or, as far as the political right is concerned, desirable.

A fear of conflict also means that the principle of unity becomes, by default, an absolute value overriding all other considerations. This is particularly dangerous during wars between nation states, sometimes roundly condemned by Rome, when national unity is added to the equation. Bishops' conferences find it extremely difficult to break step, whether through genuine pastoral concern for national troops in the field, sincere conviction that it is a 'just war', or merely over-identification of the religious with the national community, and fear of losing credibility in the national forum. The pastoral concerns for British troops in the Gulf War motivating Cardinal Hume's stance and Pope John Paul II's prophetic condemnation of this war, illustrate this dilemma.

Lack of an agreed method for analysis and action was also a recurrent problem in reaction to national democratic movements in the 1970s and 1980s when they seriously began to challenge structures of injustice, and confronted the powerful and privileged. Thus the Church in recent times has been unequivocal about racial justice and the rights of indigenous peoples, and has struggled to defend them. Likewise in Zaire, Cameroon, Malawi and Kenya it has fearlessly spoken out against state corruption and abuses of human rights. But it has been far less sure-footed, except at a distance through Catholic development agencies in the Third World, when it came to sponsoring movements through which urban workers, blacks,

Revisiting Catholic Social Teaching

indigenous people and peasants exerted power on the state and local authorities. Bishop Samuel Ruiz of Chiapas in Mexico in his support for the indigenous people of his diocese is notable as one of the exceptions to be found around the world. The papal representative attempted to have him removed in 1993. The existence of an armed struggle usually exacerbates matters. The crisis in the national development agency of the Philippines' bishops in the late 1980s is another case in point.[11]

South Africa was not an exception to this rule, but did show Catholic bishops at their most purposeful in the political arena. The bishops moved from verbal denunciations of apartheid to increasing levels of confrontation with government. Archbishop Denis Hurley, profoundly influenced by the second Vatican Council at which he participated, was ready to go to the brink of imprisonment over the injustice of South Africa's illegal occupation of Namibia.

The bishops moved from a commitment to seek redress for human rights violations to qualified support for the popular democratic movement. The Catholic secretariat in Pretoria was burnt out in reprisal. As in Rhodesia, racist legislation and repression by the state shut down consensus approaches to change. The Church learnt from, and learnt to live with, the confrontational strategy and empowerment of a mass movement, with young activists creating a bridge with the bishops.

As far as women's movements are concerned, the gap between teaching and practice, and the fear of empowerment, have in some countries created an impasse of scandalous proportions. Statements from the Holy See have been clear on the equality of women, condemnation of violence against women, and the need for equal opportunities in education and training to provide access to decision-making bodies. This only highlights the most pressing problem of justice within the Church. The lack of authority accorded women, and indeed all members of the laity, shows no sign of being taken as seriously as the situation warrants by Church leadership. The problem is, of course, worse in Third World countries where women's labour is comparatively more exploited than in the North and this exploitation is often underpinned by a *macho* Catholic culture. This remains an outstanding question-mark hanging over the authenticity and relevance of Catholic social teaching in the 1990s.

Conclusion

Many people reflect on questions of social justice only when an injustice, that may be common, is done to them personally. 'I worked for that firm for 20 years and look how I was treated' may become a moment in which political allegiances are changed and new insights about the rights of workers are given. This means that the poor, who suffer disproportionately from injustice, frequently have a far greater awareness and understanding of social justice than the rich. The food riots of the late 18th and early 19th century in Europe, for example, were sparked in Britain by those who had retained a mediaeval christian understanding of food as a means of life that should be fairly priced, 'common goods' rather than a commodity in a free market. Their 'life theology' and moral economy had survived centuries in the collective consciousness of the poor.

The Church's social teaching has meant that generations of Catholics learnt in their catechism that depriving workers of their wage was 'a sin crying out to heaven', strong words that stick in the mind long after. From the top forms of Catholic schools young people who are not necessarily poor, nor victims of injustice, have emerged with, at least, the knowledge that there exists a framework of social morality and that answers to questions of social conduct need not be made up as they go along, at the whim of the latest fad or ideology, arbitrarily resolved by reference to individual conviction alone. They have often taken this skeleton of knowledge, when it was not adequately developed in the Church, and sometimes when it was, into political parties, movements of the left and trade unions where it was built on and fleshed out.

At best they have come away with the general principles of the Church's organic tradition: the value and dignity of the worker, the idea of the common good that implies the welfare of all and the just distribution of the world's resources, the duty of the state to provide conditions in which people may live freely, responsibly and with respect for their cultures and communities, and a sense that the market must be tempered by laws and social controls in the interests of the weak and in solidarity with the poor. For some, the set of Catholic priorities that place the rights of workers and the common good above that of capital and private property have been the beacon for a life-long political commitment. For others, mostly in the countries of the Third World, it has qualified them for prison.

While it is true that this tradition is complex and reveals during its history different tendencies, and therefore requires interpretation, it is untrue that this leaves Catholics with unlimited choices about the kind of society they should strive to live in, or the socio-economic and political systems that they can find morally acceptable. Any impartial reading of this tradition, for example, would leave British Catholics in no serious doubt that the European Social Chapter should be signed. Though it often happens that ideas from this tradition, like 'subsidiarity' that appeared in the context of the defence of civil society against totalitarian encroachments by the state, may be taken out of context, distorted and used in ways that are not strictly valid.

The development of this tradition may, like a broad river, show eddies, odd currents and stagnant pools, and carry a lot of historical detritus along in it, but it has direction and contours. Its biblical bed does not permit it to meander too far off course, and its main theological current, a preference for the poor and the weak in society, drives it into conflict with the rich and the powerful both inside and outside the Church. If this broad river were to be given a single title today it would have to be the cumbersome but resonant 'option for the poor'.

It cannot be merely assumed under present conditions that the collective Catholic consciousness of social morality that informed the conscience of many in previous generations will be sustained. Modern society is too fragmented, too subject to sophisticated means of mass communication, for any romantic certainty that truth will out. Moral confidence and individual responsibility are draining away. The 'subversive memory of the poor' of a history and values in opposition to the powerful is not guaranteed always and under all circumstances to be infallible. This is a major challenge to the Church in the 1990s that many Catholic development agencies and a few Church leaders from the Third World are seriously taking up. But this is not enough.

The 'post-modern condition', the global dominance of a single economic model, neo-liberalism and its more socialised variants, the collapse of communism and the rise of ethnic nationalism in Europe, the future impact of information technology on society, all cluster around the turn of the millenium as a radically new context for the Church's social teaching. Can this organic tradition respond beyond a few simple moral injunctions? Is not the pace of social change too rapid for the lengthy deliberations of a Church which still believes that it thinks 'in the perspective of eternity'?

What is equally worrying is that social teaching emanating from Rome appears unwilling to acknowledge that it might share in its doctrinal insights anything with other christians. Or indeed acknowledge any other sources at all except the papal tradition. The Vatican's refusal to follow up a joint European meeting in Basle and co-sponsor the World Council of Churches world meeting on Justice, Peace and the Integrity of Creation in Seoul reflected this tendency. It is not as if the Catholic Church has a monopoly of insights and wisdom.

The fears that lie behind today's hiatus between teaching and practice, the lack of urgency, and resistance to change, are ultimately rooted in a lack of faith. It is worth heeding the psalm: 'the law of God gives wisdom to the simple'. The riches of the Church's social teaching will remain locked up unless the Vatican and bishops have faith in the Church of the Poor which awaits their leaderhip. They need today more than ever to see the option for the poor as a challenge to take up their teaching responsibility courageously and face the inevitable conflicts and complexities that lie on their path, and on the path of all who seek justice and peace. For them not to do so at this critical juncture in human history would be a tragedy.

Fortunately this is not the last word as far as the Church is concerned. One of the consequences of Catholic social teaching — formally so since *Octogesima Adveniens* — has been the way lay christians have been

Back to Basics

mandated to rise to the challenges of modern society and have been encouraged to do so by Church leaders. The professional expertise of the laity in this sphere is fully recognised. What is lacking is a full sense that this work of evangelisation is nothing more nor less than the *Church* fulfilling its mission, not a peripheral activity safely vouchsafed the laity while the 'real' — clerical — work of the Church is carried out elsewhere. This fidelity of the laity to the Church's mission, expressed in countless lay-led organisations and basic christian communities around the world, this bold quest for the oneness of the Church beyond the false coinage of a superficial unity, is a wealth that Church leaders must not idly squander.

Notes
1. The author would particularly like to thank Rev Donald Dorr for providing in his *Option for the Poor* (Gill & McMillan, 1992) both a template and an inspiration for this booklet, and for his help in refining the text. The views expressed are, of course, the responsibility of the author alone. CIIR would like to thank all who have commented critically on the text and offered their insights in its preparation. For further reading we recommend Cafod's *Proclaiming Justice and Peace* (1991) and, for schools, *Taking Sides* (1994), a teaching pack.
2. Understood in the sense not of being incapable of improvement but of a self-sufficient community which had all the means at its disposal to achieve its ends.
3. The *cristeros* in 1928 fought in a brutal war against a nationalist anti-clerical government that was severely repressing the Church.
4. The 'see-judge-act' method involves a cyclical process of social inquiry, analysis, reflection and action in groups.
5. By 1950, for example, 60 out of 146 bishops, and 2,500 out of 5,500 priests, were Chinese.
6. Pope John XXIII died of cancer during the Council so that Pope Paul VI presided over the session that began in September 1964.
7. 'Natural law' according to Aquinas is 'nothing other than the light of understanding infused in us by God, whereby we understand what must be done and what must be avoided', in other words what makes human behaviour into *moral* action. Unfortunately, this vision of 'natural law' as a training manual for humanity became translated during the 19th century into a rigid rule-book. The problem with the — other — biblical approach is that the Church, using Scripture, cannot claim to be talking to those for whom the Bible is not a sacred book.
8. Bishops are the heads of dioceses which are divided into parishes led by parish priests under their authority. In the period under consideration, these 'clerical' roles are contrasted in Church teaching with the 'secular' roles of the vast majority of Catholics whom they serve, called the 'laity'.
9. The present pope, of course, is also *theoretically* against the politicisation of trade unions, despite Solidarnosc.
10. A philosophy that begins in the primacy of action and the unity of the human person — for christians, 'the principal route that the Church must travel' because the mystery that is the human person is only revealed in God.
11. In the 1980s, the development agency of the bishops' conference in the Philippines, which had acted with a degree of autonomy, was taken under tight episcopal control. It had come under suspicion of channelling some monies preferentially to organisations under control of the illegal and insurgent National Democratic Front which was the political arm of the New People's Army (NPA).

Chronology

1848	*Communist Manifesto* published. Ozanam, founder of the St Vincent de Paul Society, speaks out in favour of 'revolutionary democracy' in French Second Republic.
1863-67	Publication and circulation of Marx's major theoretical texts.
1878-1903	Pope Leo XIII's pontificate.
1886	De Mun forms Association Catholique de la Jeunesse Catholique which evolves into the first Catholic trade union in France.
1891	*Rerum Novarum*.
1903-14	Pope Pius X — 'Catholic Action'.
1914-22	Pope Benedict XV.
1922-39	Pope Pius XI.
1926	'Action Française' banned. Young Christian Workers begins.
1929	*Divini Illius Magistra*.
1931	*Quadragesimo Anno*.
1933	Concordat with Nazi Germany.
1937	Encyclicals on atheistic communism and on the Church in Germany.
1939-58	Pope Pius XII.
1947-49	Persecution of church in eastern Europe.
1948	First general assembly of the World Council of Churches.
1949	People's Republic of China formed. Decree condemning all support for communism.
1952	Brazilian bishops first meet as national conference.
1956	20th Congress of CPSU condemns Stalin.
1957	*Fidei Donum*. Ghana becomes independent.
1958-63	Pope John XXIII.
1959	Castro comes to power in Cuba.
1961	*Mater et Magistra*.
1962	Second Vatican Council opens.
1963	*Pacem in Terris*.
1963-78	Pope Paul VI.
1965	*Gaudium et Spes* — Council document on Church in the modern world.

1967	*Populorum Progressio.*
1968	Medellín conference.
1971	*Octogesima Adveniens. Justice in the World*, synod of bishops. *A Theology of Liberation* published in Lima by Gustavo Gutiérrez.
1973	Paris peace accords on Vietnam.
1974-75	Victory of liberation armies in Angola and Mozambique.
1975	*Evangelii Nuntiandi.* United States withdraws from Vietnam.
1978	Pope John Paul I.
1978	Pope John Paul II.
1979	Puebla conference. Sandinista revolution in Nicaragua. *Redemptor Hominis.*
1980	*Dives in Misericordia.*
1981	*Laborem Exercens.*
1983	US bishops' pastoral on peace. Pope's visit to Nicaragua.
1984	First instruction on liberation theology.
1985	Kairos document in South Africa.
1986	Single European Act. 27th Congress of the CPSU begins perestroika process. Second instruction on liberation theology. US bishops' pastoral on economic justice.
1987	*Sollicitudo Rei Socialis.*
1988	Apostolic letter on dignity of women.
1989	Collapse of communism in eastern Europe. Basle World Ecumenical Conference on Justice, Peace and Integrity of Creation.
1990	Sandinistas defeated at polls.
1991	*Centesimus Annus.* Soviet Union disintegrates.
1992	Santo Domingo conference.
1993	Single European market formed. Papal condemnations of extreme nationalism. *Veritatis Splendor.*
1994	Synod of African bishops. Universal franchise elections in South Africa and El Salvador.